GRAMPS AND L.D.

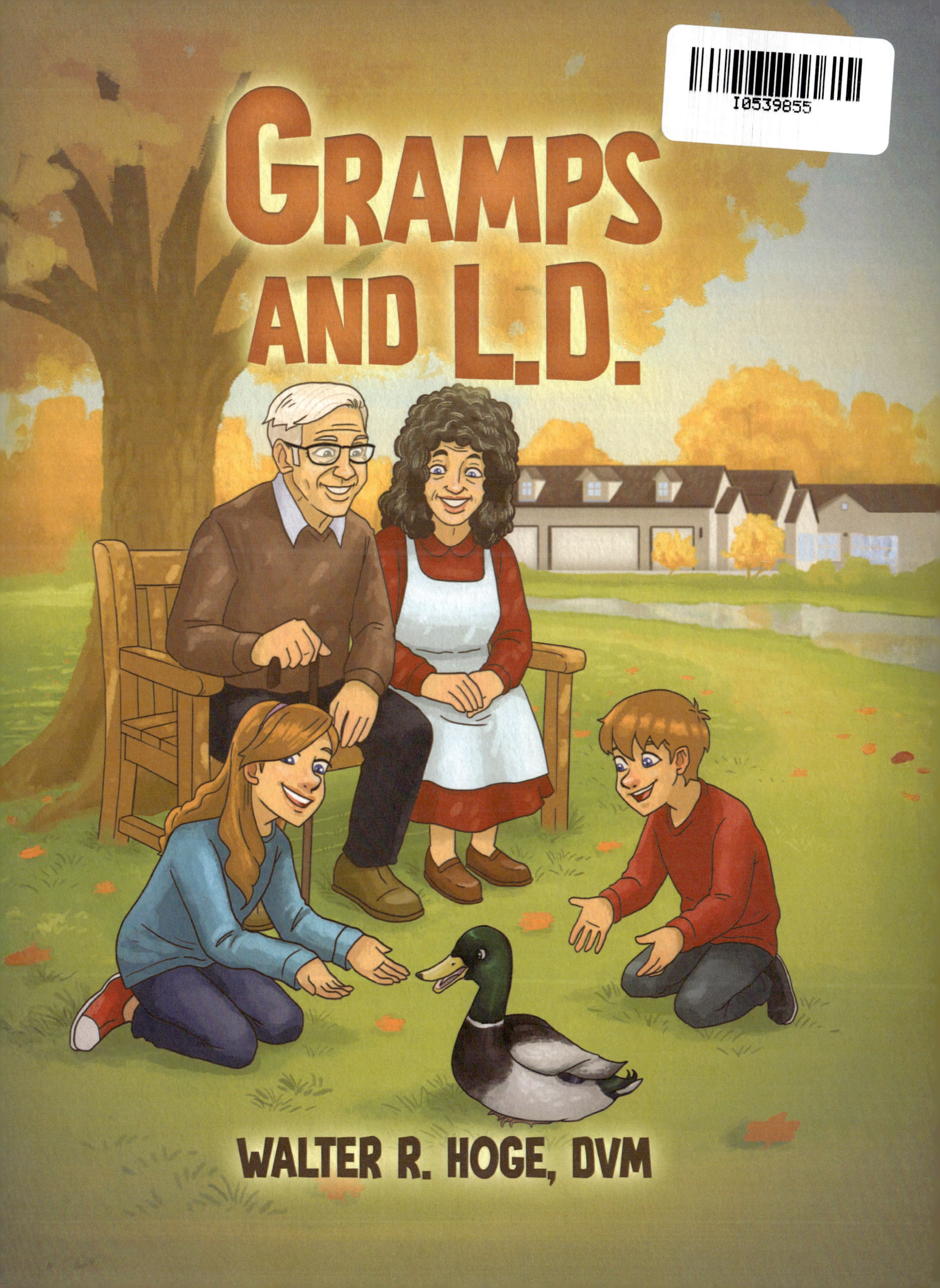

WALTER R. HOGE, DVM

Printed in the United States of America

ISBN 979-8-89114-232-9 (sc)
ISBN 979-8-89114-233-6 (hc)
ISBN 979-8-89114-234-3 (e)

Library of Congress Preassigned Control Number: 2025922167

2025.10.14

MainSpring Books
5901 W. Century Blvd
Suite 750
Los Angeles, CA, US, 90045

www.mainspringbooks.com

BASED ON A TRUE STORY.

Even though L.D. was not long with us, he touched our hearts, and we were moved by his efforts to overcome physical defects and be part of his family. He failed, but my wife, Shauna, challenged me to write about L.D., what I dreamed he could become, and the influence he would have had on our family. I hope this book will touch your heart as L.D. did ours and that even when faced with immense suffering, one can maintain faith and trust that our Heavenly Father knows us and will not ask us to do more than we can endure.

Chris and his two children (Jenny-12 and Tim-8) finally passed over into the valley where Chris was raised. The surrounding hills had changed from lush green sprinkled with wildflowers to a dull brownish gold color. The pockets of bushes and trees showed shades of red, yellow, and brown, signaling that summer was changing to fall and winter was not far off.

Chris turned his car off the familiar highway onto a lane that led down a hill and onto a bridge, where he stopped the car. "OK, kids," he points up the creek and comments, "Looks like where the creek runs around Gramps and Grandma's ranch is still low and should be safe if you want to get in. However, I would recommend you wear your sneakers to prevent cuts from sharp objects in the mud and crayfish from pinching your toes. And, Tim, remember the frogs that scared you last year when they jumped from the bushes into the water?"

Jenny jumps in with a smile on her face and adds, "Tim, watch where you get into and out of the water. I'm sure there are still ticks in the bushes and garter snakes on the bank!" Tim replies, "I wasn't scared last year reaching for a stick when I was getting out of the creek! Even though it turned out to be a slithering fat mama snake. Jenny- leave me alone!"

Chris then points down the creek. "Do not go down the creek on this side of the bridge towards the pond! I don't care what Gramps says or if he goes with you – stay away from this area! As you have been told a thousand times before, there is poison oak in the area, and we almost lost your uncle Brad in that pond. I don't want your mom to not let you stay with Gramps and Grandma before our yearly Family Reunions in the future. Gramps and Grandma need and enjoy your coming a few days before everyone else shows up for two weeks, causing confusion and stress. It also never hurts to help them out. They aren't getting any younger."

They crossed the bridge and drove towards the ranch house. Leaves were lifted and scattered towards the side of the lane as the car passed over them. They pulled up to the front of the ranch house as the door flew open with Gramps supported by a cane and Grandma with a flowered apron on, and, of course, big smiles were present on each of their faces. Jenny and Tim flew out of the car, running to their favorite grandparents. The greeting was short-lived as Chris approached his parents. The kids ran through the house, out the back, and off to visit one of their best friends.

The back door screen made a loud banging noise as an out-of-breath Jenny, followed by Tim, ran through the ranch house and confronted Gramps. "Where is L.D.?" Jenny blurts out. "The dog run door is open, and we can't find him. We checked along the creek!" Tim pipes in, "We even went to the pond where dad told us not to go looking for him. Gramps, can you please help us find him?"

A sleepy-eyed Gramps sitting in his rocking chair replies, "Now, now – just relax and let me get this old body full of rheumatism going and I'll help you find him." He slowly gets up with the aid of his cane. They go out the squeaky old screen door, and he gently closes it. From the kitchen, Grandma hollers, "That's better! I don't want to try to find another screen door for this old house!"

They walk from the patio to a sidewalk that leads to the old dog run. Jenny and Tim impatiently follow "slow old Gramps," who, with effort, takes each step. Tim impatiently says, "It's going to be dark before we can look at areas we've already been!" Gramps replies, "I wasn't born yesterday. Be patient. I know what I'm doing."

Gramps walks right past the dog run and slowly towards the creek. He walks around a bush and points with his cane towards a raised area on the bank and says, "Go ahead and look around that elevated area on the bank of the creek. I'll catch up."

When Gramps arrives, Jenny is staring at him with her hands on her hips and says, "There is no L.D. to be found! The only thing on the creek bank are these two old sticks stuck in the ground." Gramps replies, "You have found L.D." They gasp for breath, and tears flow from their eyes. Gramps goes over to a nearby bench and sits down. Jenny and Tim follow him and sit down in the grass next to the bench. Still in tears, Jenny, in a complaining voice, says, "No one has ever told me anything about L.D. I don't even know what L.D. stands for or why he died?" Gramps responds, "It's quite a long story. However, if you will be patient with me and take the time to listen, I'm sure my old body can tolerate the bench long enough for L.D.'s story." Jenny and Tim each blurt out, "Please oh please oh please - Gramps, we want to know!"

"L.D. passed away from what I believe was old age. Ducks have been documented as living for up to 26 years. As far as I can remember, I found the eggs he was hatched from at least 20 years ago." "Eggs? You never told us anything about eggs," Jenny blurted out! Gramps replied, "Might ask your parents about it. However, I question if they were ever told. It's been a long time ago. Young as they were, they probably had more important things on their minds." Tim breaks in and says, "Tell us the story from the beginning." Gramps replies, "The whole story from the beginning?" "Yes," they both reply.

"During one midsummer day, I was cutting wild grass with my tractor along the highway near home to use as a fire prevention border for our creek and home. I lifted the mower higher than usual in hopes of saving some of the wildflowers to provide seeds for the next spring. The mower passed over an area of very high grass near the brush and tree line next to the creek. I noticed a mother hen duck fly away from the area, and several black crows and a California Turkey Vulture congregated in the area. The duck returned and landed on what I guessed to be a nest. She stood there and threatened the crows and vulture until they backed off from the area and waited.

When my tractor came closer, I lifted my arms in the air and yelled, 'Get away!'. The birds left, and the mother duck crouched down until she appeared to disappear in the area. I believe she was protecting her young and keeping them warm. I got off the tractor, the mother duck flew away, and I discovered a nest with eight beautiful light brown eggs. What was I going to do? Crush the eggs to prevent the baby birds inside from suffering as birds pecked holes in the shells to eat them? Were there really any live ducklings in the eggs? Feeling guilt about what I had done, I sat on the tractor for several minutes, going over and over the options I had for these eight eggs.

My thoughts turned to an experience I had had with my mother over 70 years before. She built a small square box, placed a light bulb through a hole in one side, and a shallow pan with water on the bottom. She then turned on the light bulb, carefully placed several white eggs on the bottom, and partially closed a lid over most of the opened upper box. She then told me that the eggs were fertile, and if I would gently roll them on a regular basis, in about 21 days, we could watch baby chickens hatch from the eggs.

I turned the eggs several times each day and spent time imagining what it would be like to watch a living chick push its way into the world. Near the expected event, Mom pointed out to me a very small area of an egg where there was a small hole. She announced it was time for the chicks to be born. I watched and watched as the chicks struggled within their eggs. First, there was a bulging area in the shell. That eventually fell away. Then, I could see movement inside, and if I looked closely, the eggs would move from side to side. More shells fell away, and the chicks struggled, rested, and struggled again.

I wanted so much to help the chicks by removing some of the shell. Mom said, 'Don't help or the chick will not gain enough strength to survive. God knows that all animals, including us, must have struggles in life to gain strength and confidence to succeed.' Mother was right! It seemed like an eternity to me, but finally all the chicks slid out of their shells and lay on their sides, breathing hard. Their soft, fluffy down feathers seemed to stick to the skin as they dried. I watched them gain their strength, stand on their feet, and peck at their down feathers until they became fluffy. I wanted to feed them, but Mom told me that they do not eat usually for at least one day. This is to let all the chicks gain enough strength to follow their mothers where they could find food."

"My decision was made. I gently placed the eight eggs in my jacket and took them home. I then shined the most powerful flashlight I had through the eggs to see if it looked like they contained a live duckling. All I could see was an air pocket in one end of each egg. The rest of the area was too dense to see through. I had no idea if the eggs were fertile, had the hen been brooding (setting on her eggs), or were any of them alive. I placed the eggs in a moist towel at the bottom of a small, mostly covered plastic container. An electric heating pad was placed under the box, and I rolled the eggs as often as I could. I found that the ideal temperature to incubate duck eggs was 100 degrees Fahrenheit. I measured their temperature with an infrared thermometer. I would check the temperature each time I rolled them and moved the eggs around until they were all near the ideal temperature. I found that the ideal humidity for incubating eggs was 50% and during hatching 60%. I had no way of measuring the humidity. I closed and opened the lid to control the temperature and humidity. I ordered an automatic egg incubator, but it took six days before it arrived. When it came, there was nothing I needed to do but just sit back and look for hatching peck marks in the eggs. The incubator also had a booklet that gave suggestions on successfully hatching eggs.

Four days later, the ducklings started to hatch. It took 24 hours for seven of the eight eggs to hatch. The first egg that started to hatch was the last one to emerge from the shell. It was also the largest duckling--recovered the slowest and couldn't control his feet to walk. He would move around by using the heel of his legs. The large webs of his feet looked frozen closed and could not be used. Attempts to teach him to swim were a complete failure. He would turn over like a top and could not right himself."

Jenny interrupts and says, "Gramps, was that L.D.?" "Yes. Uncle Bob often took care of him and used the name L.D. I didn't like the name and never told anyone what it meant, except Grandma." Tim asks, "What does L.D. mean?" Gramps replies, "Lame Duck. And I'll tell you more if you keep that name to yourselves. I'll also tell you the new name we gave L.D." They cross their hearts and say scout's honor!

"L.D. mostly dragged his legs underneath him and wiggled his body back and forth with his heels under him. He became weaker and weaker. Grandma and I thought we were going to lose him. However, things improved when we found that he wasn't able to get his head high enough to drink water from the bowl. When held to the water bowl for a few days, he learned to drink water on his own. To reduce competition, we isolated him from his siblings. He got stronger and began eating mealworms, commercial duck diet, and grit (small rocks) to aid in digestion. He did not like being isolated, and after a few days, we placed a 'slow doer' in with him. With help from us, he grew up to be a beautiful drake duck. At ten months of age, the feathers grew into vibrant colors: an emerald-green head, a white neck ring, reddish breast plumage, and a curly central tail feather known as a drake feather. When L.D. died, I saved his drake feather and kept it in my bedroom nightstand. I get it out when I've had a tough day or lonely moments. Sometimes, I fall asleep with the feather in my hand and have to look all over the bedroom to find his feather.

He helped Grandma and I adjust to our eventual family empty nest and the aging changes that make our lives more of a challenge. He would fly for short distances if he could land on the grass, but never in water. I now use a cane, walk for only short distances, and, like L.D., don't swim.

The other ducklings were doing just what they were born to do. It wasn't long before they were placed outside during the day, and eventually, the old dog run became their home. They were getting bigger and bigger. Their feathers got longer and longer. It wasn't long until I left open the dog run door and put food out for them twice a day. At first, they all came for dinner, and in the late fall, they stopped coming. I hoped they were working their way south for the winter. Only L.D. became a permanent resident of our family."

"That duck meant so much to Grandma and me. He helped start our family reunions because his family stopped off at the ranch during their yearly migrations going south for the winter. L.D.'s family grew just as our family has. In fact, we scheduled our Annual Family Reunion one week before Thanksgiving to one week after, matching the time L.D.'s family started arriving at the ranch house's creek, pond, and near the old dog run. We started having such large gatherings that we conducted a lottery to determine which family would check for migrating ducks congregating near our ranch. The lottery-winning family's children's duties were to take turns placing food in the areas where the ducks were expected and scouting for them. When ducks were found, they would run to the ranch house porch and turn the crank of the fire/ dinner alarm. I must say, the children often enjoy pulling pranks by setting off the alarm with no ducks in the area. Some families place a guard at the alarm day and night to prevent pranksters from sounding false alarms. Grandma and I tell complainers it adds to the fun and helps us learn to work together. So, get over it!"

As L.D.'s and our families grew, our enthusiasm for our Annual Family Reunion grew. Without L.D., Grandma and I seem to be feeling more of the changes of aging. We are in hopes that L.D. and our family will continue to stop by the ranch once a year, even after we are gone.

L.D. taught me so much, I likened him to Job and Paul in the Bible. They both taught about suffering, faith, and God's plan for us all. Even in the face of immense suffering, one can maintain faith and trust in our Heavenly Father. Hardship doesn't always indicate punishment. It is important to have patience and compassion with ourselves and others when dealing with the limitations of life. There is a plan, and we can find joy during all phases of our lives. Grandma and I secretly changed L.D.'s name from Lame Duck to Lord's Disciple - which he was to us. L.D. took his struggles in stride and seemed to be a little better the more challenges he faced. I was grateful for the day I uncovered the duck eggs so many years ago, and for remembering my mother showing me how to incubate chicken eggs. Lord's Disciple has made such a difference in our family. I hope and pray that L.D.'s family continues to stop at the ranch for rest and a bite of food on their way south for the winter year after year. I also hope that L.D.'s family will influence my family to continue having Annual Family Reunions at the ranch."

And they did. Year after year, Gramps's and Grandma's ranch accommodates larger and larger numbers at their Annual Family Reunion. And yes! The ducks during the week before and after Thanksgiving accumulate in increasing numbers at the ranch's pond, creek, and near the old dog run. Large amounts of food are scattered in those areas – especially near where L.D. made his home in the dog run near the ranch house where Gramps and Grandma for so many years lived with their beloved L.D.

Also, food is spread on the raised area near the creek, where a cross marks where L.D. was buried. It was placed there as a reminder that L.D. was never able to swim. Near the bench, a monument has been placed which reads: In dedication to L.D.'s consistent positive attitude with no complaints. For his constant example of looking for the best, no matter what came our way. He has endured much; his family gives him honor by yearly visits to our ranch during the Thanksgiving Holiday Season, and most of all, L.D., you have had a never-ending influence of love on Gramps's and Grandma's family. You creatures of our God and King – come eat and rest a spell before you continue on your journey...All is well. Forever thankful for our L.D. *Gramps & Grandma.*

There are now three crosses on that raised area near the creek that bears L.D.'s name and the two who helped him as he helped them. All faced the creek that none of them had ever been able to swim in.